Cutthroats

and Other Poems

Cutthroats
and Other Poems

by Ted Dyck

TURNSTONE PRESS

Cutthroats and Other Poems

Turnstone Press
Artspace Building
206-100 Arthur Street
Winnipeg, MB
R3B 1H3 Canada
www.TurnstonePress.com

MIX
Paper from responsible sources
FSC® C016245

Turnstone Press gratefully acknowledges the assistance of the Canada Council for the Arts, the Manitoba Arts Council, the Government of Canada through the Canada Book Fund, and the Province of Manitoba through the Book Publishing Tax Credit and the Book Publisher Marketing Assistance Program.

Printed and bound in Canada by Friesens for Turnstone Press.

Library and Archives Canada Cataloguing in Publication

Dyck, E. F., author

Cutthroats & other poems / Ted Dyck.

ISBN 978-0-88801-501-3 (pbk.)

I. Title. II. Title: Cutthroats and other poems.

PS8557.Y38C88 2014 C811'.54 C2014-904437-2

For Robert Kroetsch

CONTENTS

Dedication

I went to the University of Manitoba in the fall of '75 to study with Robert Kroetsch Months earlier he had read in Moose Jaw where I was then teaching mathematics from one of those rants in *The Words of My Roaring* He would be interesting to work with I thought So when I met him later that night at a party in Regina hosted by a co-member of the Moose Jaw Movement I chatted him up Yes, he would consider being my advisor How did I know about Russian formalism anyway—and would I be interested in reviewing Dorn's *Gunslinger* for *boundary 2* I had never heard of the man or the magazine so I said yes Great, he said I'll send you the book and he turned away to a lovely twenty-something waiting impatiently for me to finish

Everything I know about RK is contained in that episode

He was a writer of astonishing range and vitality He was also a man of great even foolish generosity He had a passion for and a powerful effect on beginning writers He was a diffident PhD advisor acting only to prevent me from making a fool of myself He was disappointed by my rejecting postmodernism but I had studied contemporary logic

His was the most important influence on my writing life

WRITING THE CUTTHROAT

Usually you begin with a thought. Cutthroat, then, and at once you hear/see a doubled memory, a splash/flash of red missing a grey Adams fly on a bright summer's day, above the treeline, in a high mountain stream running cold over the bright stones. But this is the idea of your thought; it is not your thought itself. Your thought is already deeper in the pool; your thought is the cutthroat, now out of sight and sound, over which the grey fly of your idea floats uselessly. The cutthroat is gone, and it will not rise, though you continue to cast, as you have learned, perfectly and carefully arching the weight of your line, with its weightless idea at the far end, out over the pool. You turn away, leaving that final cast to itself, and just then the trout strikes—you have it—but you set the hook too quickly, and it is gone again. You have not landed your cutthroat. The trout nearly caught is not the trout you desire. The idea is not the thought.

You feel doubled. Perhaps you should write about the fishing, and not about the fish. What do you really know about the cutthroat, after all? All you know is about the attempt to catch the damned thing, and even that seems doubtful. If the art of fishing were really known to you, or so you reason, you would already have caught the trout. Yet now your hand is tensing, as though it were gripping the muscular, jumping body of a living cutthroat. Perhaps you do know something about fish after all. But you are uneasy; something is troubling you.

On a sunny day you have seen cutthroat feeding in the deep pool, just below a narrow, rocky channel called "The Chute," a kilometre downstream from where Ranger Creek joins the South Ram River. One will float up from the depths, you remember now, and, if the fly looks interesting, the trout will rush it, turning, at the moment of the strike, like an Olympic swimmer. That's when you feel the trout first, that's the hit. The hit is followed by a sustained pull—or your line goes slack. Only later do you register the flash of colour if it's a miss, or see the red belly and the slash along the lower jaw if it's a catch, and that's when you start looking for a stone.

You're not sure you feel any better. Perhaps it's time to mention the mayfly on which the trout feeds and which the artificial flies are said to imitate. You have actually caught one or two of these Ephemeroptera, in late evening, as they were surging their way into the trees for the night. Their only night, it turns out, for they live only twenty-four hours in the insect stage, maturing, mating, laying their eggs, and dying without feeding once. They don't even have jaws. It's a short life—and that thought jumps in your mind like a trout—what are you doing, wasting time, writing about flies when your thought is the cutthroat and life is so short?

You resolve not to be diverted. You will return to the cutthroat. A green-backed trout with a flushed belly, just the right size for a pan—and, yes, you have fried them fresh out of the cold, clean streams, in butter and onions, nothing else. You have cut the cooked flesh along the back, peeling the upper fillet away from the backbone, then lifting the spine, whole, from the lower fillet. You have washed the flaked meat down with brandy, with Fundador. But that thought just now does not please you. It's like the mayfly business, which was like the living trout in your hand—diversions, you say to yourself—that's it—focus on cutthroat. Nothing else.

But the trout is still gone and you go to your maps, the big topographic maps on the wall of your study. Your finger remembers the main artery of the South Ram, pauses on the spot where you remember catching your first cutthroat, moves past your first camp, on toward where you now camp, further upstream from that spot, then west past the vein of Hummingbird Creek, on to Ranger, and further, to Lost Guide Lake where golden trout can no longer be found. Everything is changing along the South Ram. When you first arrived seven years ago, almost no one camped where you did. You could go for days, seeing hardly another human. Now it's all dust and noise and All Terrain Vehicles with overweight riders, and young, stupid fathers teaching their sons how to shoot across a river at a mountain. It's horse trailers and house trailers, horseshit and human shit—everywhere.

But you want to return to the trout, to your thought. You don't want to think about the end of the South Ram as you have learned to know it. You don't want to think about the short life of the mayfly, though without the mayfly the trout is dead. You don't want to think of eating the trout, or of any of the things that distract you from your thought. For a moment—a split moment—you wonder if your thought is really about the cutthroat at all, but you put that thought out of your mind.

So you cast again, hoping that your idea will catch your thought, that the grey fly will lure the trout, that technique will raise the living thing hidden in its deep pool. You cast and you cast—but there is no hit. You cast and cast—and you feel worse and worse. You are standing at the edge of that swirling pool. You can sense the fish deep below you. They rise, curious about the false fly; they sink, without attacking. Vertigo. How many times have you stood here and wondered about all the others who have stood here before you? You strip more line from your reel and you cast again, but now to the far side of the pool. It occurs to you that just as you will—you hope—wash the cooked trout down with brandy, just so will you someday be eaten. Death. You reel in some line and cast again, shorter now, to the calm spot beyond the first eddy. Above you, you remember, someone is remembered, the spot marked by a simple, wooden cross. Someone's father. Someone who loved this spot as you do, someone who worked this river, this pool, patiently and carefully. You keep casting. Your arm is getting tired.

And it does happen, again. You let the line and fly float—and at that moment, as so often before, the trout, risen from the bottom and hidden behind a rock, strikes. The muscles in your arms register its twisting, living attack, and as you set the hook, properly this time, as your split-cane rod arches and nearly doubles, as the adrenalin pumps into your blood, you see that the trout you have been seeking, the thought now openly struggling near the surface, is not a cutthroat at all. This trout is the birth of the end of the West Country; it is the life of the mayfly on which the cutthroat feeds; the blow of stone on the neck of the living thing that feeds you. The name of this trout, of your thought, your desire, is the doubled name of the gods to whom you return the first trout of every season.

At last, you can admit it: the name of this trout is the name of life, the name of death, the name of love. The name of this trout is your name, its life is your life, its death yours, its love your desire.

There are, finally, no secrets: in writing the cutthroat, you have written yourself. A moment of grace was given you, you felt the urgent press of time, you stood again at the edge. The gods are merciful, even those of your invention. But be careful: the word, like the hook, can kill; the cutthroat, like you, dies by living; and the terror and beauty are not too much to bear.

The Cutthroat Poems

The Fisher

All those years of fishing cutthroat
those years of playing guitar
(years of losing his women)

Those rivers running into the sea
yet the sea never getting full
(the sea is never full)

Rivers of life
rivers of blues
(rivers of death)

Always he goes to the sea again
to search in the mouths of rivers
(mouths like running graves)

There in the mud and suck of the deltas
he hunts for his one true love
(a plastic and toxic love)

He casts to the sea-running cutthroat
a fish so burned by chemistry's love
(its throat behind the gills blood red)

He hooks that cutt on a small grey fly
he plays it to shore through the foam
(hauls it to shore through the crud)

He breaks the neck of the cutt
so beautiful, so frail, so red
(twists the body behind the head)

Cooks the fish in the open and eats it
its tender flakes poisoning his mind
(mercury pumping to his brain)

And desire is born again, Fisher
from the flesh of poison and death
(flesh so poisoned it's death)

More years of fishing cutthroat
more years of playing guitar
(years of losing his women)

In the river of life and death
river of life and death
(life and death)

Cutthroat #1

That slash on your throat, my love,
was a vicious cut to my stony heart.
When I saw you I knew you'd been hurt,
though you'd survived my hand's gloved
grasp. I was your enemy, and you loved
me more than breath or life or truth.
I knew you had kept a lover's dark faith,
and would spurn love's shade for love.
But now I know you better. Now I know
that I was the romantic one, not you,
that you were the hard-hearted lover
who could wear the doubled red choker
a necklace of rubies brokered
in love's true market, under cover.

Cutthroat #2

Sometimes you are so thinly grey
on the stones below your wraith-
like body there is no flickering shape
not even in the high-noon sun of day.
Then you are but a shade at play:
after love you will leave your mate
to his lovely grievous twisted fate.
You will laugh, and you will pray:

This is a good day for love to die.
This is a good day for love to grey.
This is a good day to claim the prize.
It's not a bad day for love to die.
It's not a bad day to turn love grey.
It's not a bad day to claim the prize.

Cutthroat #3

And sometimes you are fat as a fish
full of eggs, with the plump, red drum
of your belly sounding the beats ta-dum
ta-dum your doubled heart's wish.
When you choose the succulent crayfish
the stone-fly's nymph, both at home
in the slow current and the river foam,
and roll lazily up, the gentle swish
of your thrusting tail speaks to me:

See what you'll be losing when I go
(with my belly so red and full of roe)
to the river's source high in the scree.
My voice in answer, unbroken but low:
I will rather die than admit it's so.

Cutthroat #4

So let's play pintail on the rosy
instead of ring around the donkey.
Let's play jumping jack in boxes
instead of goose and sneaky foxes.
You know what I mean dammit
and I know that you know that
I know that you know dammit
and this won't ever bell the cat.

Wuzza fuggan rugga, I say,
& you know exactly what I mean.
Zazza fuggan rugga, you say,
& I know exactly what you mean.
It's cutthroat poker that we play,
waiting / for the waiting day.

Cutthroat #5

You're safe. The cutthroat season's done
and winter's almost here. The westerlies
are bringing snow. A late fall moon flees
across a sky patrolled by dog and huntsman.
"Thirty days in November" are left to run.
Borealis tucks his shawl about his knees,
lets his icy breath uncoil above the trees.

The river slows. The trout, stunned motion-
less, forget to feed. Yet, an idea of spring
is already born: the stream is ready to rise;
the push to spawn, still latent in your brain,
trembles along your belly, already blushing
faintly, swelling with a million fishy eyes.
You will soon be in danger, once again.

Cutthroat #6

The bell's throated knell, the cannon's chested roar
bursts like Christmas in your ear, held to the ice
of the river long before break-up. At this solstice
Cutthroat, only the Angler knows the late hour.
And the roar is only in the ear, not in the cold air
holding its breath for the birth of the fabled prince
of peace. We are always waiting for the birth, mince-
minded and puddin'-headed, for the already past hour.

Good King Angler did look out on the Feast of Stephen.
All the ice lay round about, deep and clear and even.
The cutthroat trout held still below, thin & drab & dumb.
When the bell began to toll, echoed by the cannon's thump
it rolled red belly up, by knell and dull roar driven
to birth an image for the Angler on the Feast of Stephen.

Cutthroat #7

And now it's the New Year. When I was young
I was proud to make no New Year's resolution.
Bloody fools! I didn't need a silly illusion
to kid myself (ha) that I was going to change.
Okay, so I was wrong, so what, we're all wrong
some of the time (you know the cliché) & so on.
But I've begun to wonder: Suppose illusion
is that necessary fiction (ha), suppose change
is willy-nilly—see what I mean, buddy guy?

I envy the young. Wrong-headed as they are,
they've got time on their side, & that far
far country is drawing nearer my god to me.

Ol' Cutthroat's waiting, her full belly's red.
Ol' Cutthroat's spawning, we'll all soon be dead.

Cutthroat #8

(For Zeenan, d. 1997, age 3)

The embroidery of freudery,
said Jack—speaking of egory.
The embroidery of deathery, say
I—the deathery of livingry.

You cry 'n cry alone, boy,
cuz you cryin' fo yo'se'f.
You cry 'n cry alone, boy,
cuz you dyin' soon yo'se'f.

Life is bad, but death is worse,
so said the scop of olden verse.
The grave's a fine & private place,
but none I think do there embrace.

Through your dead eyes you see nothing
of the sun on the mountains, dancing.

Cutthroat #9

I have a thing, Cutthroat, for the liturgy:
that chant, the purity of the celibates' longing,
Salve Regina in the abbey, the Virgin holding
Her son to Her breasts, black with energy.
And the Russian mass: words thick as allegory,
the tongue on the lips and the palate, lips kissing
Her lips and tongue tonguing Her mouth, praying
for mercy, hands busy under the black canopy.

Stabat Mater! Your secret love so black,
like Aphrodite your lusty Eros on your lap.
The name of love is the name of the mother,
the name of law is the name of the father.
The sad monks name your effinineffable name
Mother. Their swollen tongues utter no other.

Cutthroat #10

Like a sign in the east, the comet throbs quietly
in the morning sky, blurred by a fish-scale cloud,
paling before the rising equinoctial sun, shroud-
ed in a light greater than its own false piety.
The last comet, Cutthroat, you will ever see—
and the first. Alpha and omega, the vicious round
of the snake, its tail in its mouth, that bounds
perfectly your imperfect desire for perfect peace.

You had not thought it would begin to end like this.
You had thought you would slouch heroically toward
a waiting dragon, your puny blade ready, your shield
over your pumping heart. Lesser foes would have yielded
place to one worthy of your desire, of your rusted sword's
wish. Not this comet, this false light, this snake's hiss.

Cutthroat #11

Cutthroat, one plus one equals two, the smallest prime
integer of love. The number two-in-one, the couple,
the originary binary, the basis of figure, the double,
your other and my self, a game of mime.
Or is it hate that doubles love, as clean opposes grime?
Opposition, difference, and how to double your trouble.
Not pro but contra, the prick that breaks the bubble,
the bastard, the shadow, the necessary slide of time.

Not pan but pun [words getting on top of each other,
even if only nearly s/mother/fucking one another].
What is this figure that creeps between us between
love and hate between death and life between you
and me delaying the beginning of the end
for which we long with fear?

Cutthroat #12

When you suspect there's a cutthroat in the river
you pause carefully. You notice the slightest ripple
in the quiet pool. The least green-coloured tipple
of an arched back, breaking, will make you shiver.
The very birds fall silent. Thought of the grizzly bear
is lost. An elk cow grazing hardly notices you
or you her. You will the trout to the darkest spot, blue-
green, where you will place the fly of feathers and hair.

Now your arm whips the split-cane rod back and forth.
The long line sings; the tiny fly dries in the wind.
Now you slow your arm so the line extends above the spot
and the fly drifts slowly down to the water as the wind dies.
Now it lands. The surface holds. Will a grey shape float up-
ward to the fly? Will it take sweet death in its mouth?

Cutthroat #13

That dark spot, Cutthroat, of deep blue-green, willed
by my will to be your death—will you meet me there?
To pass up the blue-green spot on the water is not fair
trade to the one who names it, who wants you gulled
by the thing itself: Cutthroat, you know you are pulled
by the golden grey fly, are tempted by my blue-green dare.
Come: kiss the grey fly, touch your lip to the hare's
golden bristle, nibble death. Come, take, be killed.

Your body twists violently in my hand.
I marvel at the fading rose-hue of your belly,
your greenish back, the slash on your throat,
your futile thrusts, your beauty as you die.
Cutthroat, Cutthroat, you whom I love.
Cutthroat, Cutthroat, bless me from above.

Cutthroat #14 (The Golden Trout)

High in the mountains, three alpine lakes, stepped
one above the other, gleam in the thin light of the sun,
broken only by the Goldens jumping for joy and the fly,
their bellies cutthroat red, their backs as bright as gold.

I have climbed this mountain to kill you. I have
killed the Cutthroat, over and over, and now you
O Golden One, must die. I shall kill you with a fly
tied with ego and hope in grey and blue.

The mountain has been climbed, the cougar faced.
Am now I pure enough to kill my trout's desire?
—the golden, fabled, rare, and deathless trout?

I drift across the lake surface on my belly-boat,
casting the arc of my encircling desire
to be that golden trout I kill to live.

Cutthroat #15 (The Cliché Edge)

What is it then
drives me to this cliché edge—
to this face of vertigo?

That trout I hook has been caught before.
The pull on my line is as old as a mountain.
Many stand before me, here, at this edge
overlooking this swirling pool.
The neck I now break has been broken
already, and my thanks to the river gods
are a repeat   repeat   repeat   repeat.

When I lift the last morsel to my lips
I know that as I eat this holy fish
so too will I be eaten. I drink
my brandy, my blood.

Every new heart breaks as no heart
before it. The pale rose blackens
eternally on the thorn. The crescent
moon sinks forever into a curved
morning sky.

The great machine stutters,
and begins, again.

Ram River Poems

Hummingbird Creek

All the clichés are true:
sheep frolic on the mountainside,
trout splash in the cold clear stream,
black ravens wing over the steep gorge,
and bears feed languidly on the berries.
Our fire, our tent, our camp—
our nest under the north star.
Will winter never come?

The night is crisp with longing.
The Ram glistens, moonstruck
under the snow-capped peaks. Brandy
roars in my throat like a bull.
¡Olé! you cry. ¡Olé!
A horn lodges in your groin,
a knife enters my heart.
Love, I want this love, this winter.

In the brash morning sun
on a rock over the falls
you strip off your shirt.
I choose you, you say,
your breast the perfect
shape of your love. Below us
in the deep pool a cutthroat
whips his tail into a frenzy,
surges up into the rushing water.

Hummingird hummingbird.
High on a ridge—lookout.

Cutthroat

Only the mosaic of stones in the pool.
Only the clear roiling mountain water.
Only the ceaseless swirling of current.

You watch the surface for emerging flies.

The stones shine like sons of the shining sun.
The clear water reflects the colours of colour.
The current measures the endless measure of time.

You see a mayfly spinning up into the wind.

Now the roar of froth at pool's head,
the babble of water on stone at the tail,
and the wind sighing over the mountains.

Then a dark arc
a flash of red on white
Splash.

That such grace is given.

Mayfly, Mayfly

Ephemeropteron
you are birthed, matured, mated, and dead,
all in one day and no eating
though for years you live nascent
in the water
food for the cutthroat.

To mate on the wing
is quite the thing.
To die in a day
is too damn soon.

Most of your life you've slept
under a rock,
the cutthroat lurking.

So far you have escaped
that beautiful death.

Gods of the River Ram

You have given me the steely cutthroat.
You have shown me the mountain sheep.
You have hidden from me (so far) the bear
though you have shown me his clawed track.
You have hidden also the mountain cats
whose matriarch on this river is "Daisy."

You held me at the edge of the whirlpool
where I have been held before.
You walked me up & down the great rock
as I whispered, "Where are the Rockies?"
You led me to discover the sparrow's egg
orchid, delicate as a lady's slipper.
You took me to where the wild onion grows
pungent as garlic over a high alpine lake.

You have healed me when I was sick
with the privation of all pleasure.
You have heaped a scorn of hailstones
on me and thundered and flashed at me.

O gods of the river,
you who have humbled me with joy,
what do you want from me?

I walk up and down your river
and see you in every stone, every falls,
every pool, every run—waiting.

I bow down before you, I praise you.

Is it not enough that I invent you?

Red Bird & Cup

after a line by Patrick Lane

That buffalo jump in the long dry valley
summer beating down on my frightened body
and all about us the smashed skulls . . .

I place this in a paper cup for you.

That dark night filled with love, the stones
eternal in the holy river, the mountain grim
and our trembling bodies pressed together . . .

I place this in the paper cup for you.

These are my small gifts, my love,
the cup is not full, & the red bird
bears it, fragile, on his back . . .

"O Reason Not the Need"

— *King Lear* 2.4.259

I have no reason to be afraid tonight.

My dog has pressed her cold nose into my hand.
I have poured myself another snifter of brandy.

No need at all for self-pity.

The mountains are white against the black sky.
Two votive candles gutter light to write by.

I am not alone: the river gods are here with me.

In the bathroom, a leaking toilet mutters.
On the radio, sad Polish folk songs sputter.

My own words pulsate somewhere in cyberspace.

The North Star flickers in the Milky Way
The cougar's scream terrifies the fleeing hare.

Tomorrow, I hike deep into the mountains.

My sister lies under the snowy prairies.
My beloved wears a dead man's rings.

I am not afraid.

Bone Creek Blues

Bone Creek Blues

The rancher says it empties into the Frenchman River,
the guidebook says it flows into Swift Current Creek.
So—it flows into the Gulf of Mexico—or Hudson's Bay?

The RM of Bone Creek says it's just a nickname,
the Hutterite believes it names a creek in his land,
A name is just a name—or label gone astray?

The rancher thinks it's really Conglomerate Creek,
the RM rationalizes it's really Swift Current Creek.
That is—to be, or not to be?

The fisherman watches Bone Creek pooling
along its bank where the current slows
for the feeding brown trout he knows
should be rising soon in the high sun.

Nothing.

Maybe he is fishing Conglomerate Creek (one for the rancher).
Maybe he is fishing Swift Current Creek (the RM was right).
Maybe it is Bone Creek (and the Hutterites took all the trout).

He is saddened as he turns away
breaks down his rod and packs his gear:
not for the possibly missing trout,
nor for the impossibly named creek;
but for the lost place
the false truth
the true lie.

Mennomonk, the Poem

Mennomonk, the poem

1.
mennomonk laughs his wicked laugh
he smiles his wicked smile & laughs
through rotten teeth eyes open wide

mennomonk holds his head in his hands
it hurts it hurts his head his hands
he thinks it hurts his head

mennomonk never looks up but down
his wicked head in his wicked hands
his rotten teeth his wicked smile

you mennomonk you within
uh_uh uh_uh uh_uh uh_uh
yeah yeah yuck yuck

2.
ontogenesis repeats phylogenesis
ha says mennomonk that's what you think
i'll read you genesis chapter & verse

in the beginning (before the big bang) god
(a perfect mennomonk) created heaven
(where was he during this time ho) and earth

it took him six days to get to mennomonk
(created in his image of course) so much
for ontogenesis repeats phylogenesis

not to mention the problem of the garden

3.

& speaking of time, continues mennomonk, where
were you, god, before the beginning? if i can
imagine it so can you & amen   but he can't

really O my head my head mennomonk gnashes
his teeth   his rotting teeth   he spits
plop plop plop   armed men spring up

mennomonk's amazed holy cadmus he sings
in a cracked falsetto voice glory glory
he lifts his arms he closes his eyes

the fighting men fall back to earth
time turns & eats itself   farts
a little bang & wakes him up

he's back at square one he sees that
tricked again it's scratch my hairy pits
he thinks & laughs his wicked laugh

4.

now take the garden says mennomonk
there was a fulltime job no uic
all those weeds   i mean plants

& no wonder water water everywhere
& ne'er a drop to drink just apples
golden & discordant on that tree

woke up one mornin o my achin head
woke up one mornin full o pain & pride
woke up one mornin a woman by my side

i'll admit it says wicked mennomonk
i'd et a fallen apple the night before
or maybe two fell asleep & when i woke

there she was

5.

she was morn   she was night
she was dark   she was light
she was warm   she was naked

& mennomonk lost it right there

6.

& when she suggested a division of labour
(less hanky panky   no real dangers)
what could you say mennomonk eh eh

you didn't know she'd been dreaming apples
you didn't know she'd been dreaming snakes
& she was right too much hanky panky

the rose in your hand wilted
the pain in your side throbbed
flesh of your flesh

heart of your heart

7.

the snake mennomonk wasn't a red herring
one rotten apple didn't spoil the barrel
& the earth did not feel the wound

o she was high all right high as the kite
she'd been flying while you'd been weeding
her cheeks were flushed she was breathless

admit it   you couldn't stand it
ok for you to fly & dream of flying
ok for you to offer the rose

but she was lily of the valley
she was vine & you were elm
she was virgin virgin virgin

wrong you stupid mennomonk

she was black she was comely
she was virgin she was whore
she was she & she was lovely

8.

ever since he's been here mennomonk
changes changes changes everywhere
what's it all about he thinks

first the weeds
then the virgin
now the whore

he coins a word to flip in his mind
metamorph metamorph what is next
sweat pours from his aching head

another tooth falls out
the virgin/whore is pregnant
he checks his stool for signs

nothing
but more change

9.
old mennomonk has worries here
in the garden that's why his head
with worries aches that's why his
laugh is wicked

he's seen it all before & yet & yet
this time he worries it bugs him
is it round or is it straight

& the virgin sings O let's sing
& the whore cries Well do me
& mennomonk holds his head

what about the child & will
it find a mother for its tears
& what if he is not its father

now there's a good one
his head hangs down &
nothing will raise it

from the dead

10.
but it does rise, a little
resurrection from a little death
the virgin/whore's amazed

it's in his head of course (ha)
where else but his swollen aching
head it soon too soon subsides

return   return
if you're lucky, mennomonk

11.
here in the high hills his head
hurts less—it's the air, he thinks
the pure mountain air

above the abbey and the town
red roofed far below, his throat
is not so dry & he breathes

from both nostrils
first the left then the right
but wait—what's that

no stopped chant that
no pealing organ in the chapel
that ringing in his head

black virgins are singing
from the tops of mountains
their unrelenting song

their shrieking piercing song
high elah so high that mountains
fall away and rocks come crashing

down on mennomonk
holding his aching head
crying his wet tears

12.
& while you're holding your head
mennomonk, the lady with the ass
(her phrase) is casting the virgin

in her eyes over her shoulder
in a seedy motel on a street where
one behind her grunts   grunt grunt

she's on the plains, you're in the sky
she's down below, you're way up high
she bells the ball, you will not dance

she's the one mennomonk
whom you seek, whom you love.
go down, mennomonk. get dirty.

go down.

13.
or maybe he thinks next day maybe
it was monkeys screaming not virgins
singing in his aching hurting head

yes monkeys apes baboons
howlers ringtails chimpanzees
simian sisters

or maybe one big sister
you jane me hanuman
wanna make whoopee?

14.
where did monkey start he thinks
who said the primal word
and which was first

the verb
the noun
and what was said before

a smaller question than
when did time begin and
where o where and how

or is it

15.
the monkey on his back scratches
itch is everywhere & mennomonk
mennomonk scratches back

16.
why is there something
rather than nothing
mennomonk scratches back

so we could ask
that question
monkey scratches back

why must what goes up
come crashing down
mennomonk scratches back

17.

& first her mother died
& then her father died
but monkey never dies

monkey lives forever on his back
her sentence never means never dies
she lives forever goddess grammar

me dr death
die monkey die forever
in your goddam grammar

18.

like that dog in the street
swaying for days   drooling
in the soft sea breeze

catching on its ribbed body
the stones & insults of boys
catching death from angels

you mennomonk what you know 'bout death
'cept what you read 'bout death in books
'cept what you fear 'bout death

you have drooled mennomonk
you have caught stones
you have thinned & swayed

how come you aint caught death

yet

19.

remember the act of remembrance
remember everything forgetting
nothing: beautiful (not true)

remember the poppy's red lie
the midnight's blooded moon
the long (false) drive to home

remember the singing monks
her white face in the crowd
her black heart in the crowd

remember,
mennomonk? stupid?

20.
hang down yr head mennomonk
hang down yr head and cry
smash down yr head mennomonk

poor boy you want to die

21.

so you like music mennomonk
you like song you like blues
well   wail then

not for the love you lost
not for the death in birth
not for the reaper time

for the lovely illusion
for the chimera belief
for the sweet lie lost

22.

O yellow rose
& turning brown, the edges
of your petals curling

O mother, your yellow roses
watered by the sewer water
from the kitchen sink all summer
bloomed like crazy

O love, you yellow rose
feeding on garbage, your flower
in the sun brown & putrid
O *anus mirabilis*

Moment of Perfection

Moment of Perfection

Was it when you discovered a nest of sparrow's-egg orchids
high in the mountains
Or the cutthroat from the deep pool floated up to your fly and
gulped his death

Maybe at coffee and brandy in a cafe behind "The Buttocks of
God" in Augsburg
Or lying nude in the chemical sun at Baggersee burning your
fiftyish body brown

Perhaps when the night train to Berlin stopped at the border
and dogs sniffed out
Your camera bribed back from the police but the photograph
of true love was gone

Or in the chapel of the Black Virgin, the monks singing Salve
Regina, their longings
As the whores of salvation in the courtyard below at night
bared their black breasts

Perhaps much earlier: the roar of a football crowd in
Minnesota, the fall brilliant
Your new wife pregnant beside you, a lizard whose growing
will kill you and her

Go back farther: marzipan Kuchen crumbling in your mouth
on a Munich Saturday
A small lake in the Alps, Klosterwein, your Saskatchewan legs,
your Canadian feet

Or Ruth, daughter of Zacharias, love child, her hair flaming
    red, your first love
The high grandeur of her disdain from the top of the turning
    hill of your dreams

Or when Lone Feather roamed along the cut-banks of snow
    high as the willows
Peering into the white future where sky seamlessly joined snow
    at infinity

When the elephant of the night, trunk searching, trumpeted in
    awful triumph
You fleeing for your life and always barely escaping, then
    falling, then waking

To nightmare of the belt drawn from your trousers by your
    father, his face twisted
In righteous fury, the beatings, your sins, the beatings, your
    sins, beatings and sins

To the beginnings: once on a perfect morning the river-breaks
    shone in the sun
And you fell onto a stubbled field only to wail that [you] were
    born—was that it—

The perfect moment, when slowly, tenderly
The doula grasped the gravedigger's shovel?

Fuga per Canonem

Fuga per Canonem

1. Head

How to compose: strictly according to rule.
What rule: canon (by recursion).

How strictly:
It is an extraordinary thing that hardly any of the well-known treatises on fugues so much as mentions Bach because [his fugues] are "contrary to the rules."
Learn to fuga: start, soar, stop.
Oh: well: fly then, bee, to your nest.

Fly according to rule:
start (expose yourself)
soar (middle, free)
stop (go home, to start).

Fly, little ones, fly away to rest.

2. Freely

The figure of argument, the place
of places before and after
O little pair, and "love
in the western world"
the great grey muddle!

So fly, soaring slowly drawing
it out as the beaded days click
past on nobodaddy's rosary clack
flap your wings go higher higher.

Oh—sorry—you're a bee
not a bird. Buzz off.

Here a flower there a flower
everywhere a flower flower
old nobody had a flower
e i e i ooo suck the honey
slowly augment augment

Or zip around like crazy everything's contracting the world's a village and your buzz sounds in the inner chambers a wigged and pampered judge scratches his ear and the queen shifts uneasily onto the other cheek and somewhere a man whose dusky skin is many colours is shrinking he has loved many now he has slim O son of man *diminutio*

Fly upside down that's easy
down is up and wrong is right
and white is black and don't
look down I mean up

Flying upside down you crash
if you fly too high Icarus
into the earth bang it's over

To get high go down
To soar plunge
To sing weep.

Freedom is a chain so
sing in your chains like
your chains make you free.

3. Home

To *make a bee-line*, worker,
is to head straight for the hive
no playing around no suckypoo
go home and unpack your bags.

The rule (canon) is
bumble around sucking nectar
pollinate a few lucky flowers
bee-line home.

You don't *wanna go home?*
Too bad.

4. Coda (The 4th Movement, Op. 135, Beethoven)
Grave, ma non troppo tratto—Allegro

muss es sein muss es sein
es muss sein es muss sein

must it be must it be must it
must be it must be it must be

musty bee dusty bee fusty bee
it musta been it musta been it

shoulda been it shoulda been &
woulda been it woulda been if

ida been and uda been sheda been
a musty bee a fuzzy bee a busy bee

it coulda been it coulda been it
woulda been what shoulda been a

musty buzzy busy bee alive
with love bees with love bees

if love be if truth be it must be
what will be it must be it must

it be?

In Remembrance

Lament

I cannot bear it grandmother
that you born in number four village russia
peasant by birth by faith by pride
that you were let down rouged & curled &
oh so white / you were always quite brown
large moles graced your face

we bear you grandmother
your grandsons / to the grave / at the end
you did not believe we were grandsons

never believed that men
had landed on the moon / what would they
do up there you said

would not have believed
that your children who did not let you die
in their smart homes fell on your thin body
beating their breasts

you did not weep when we let
your husband down / mawk dem tau you said
(close him up) turned away on the arm
of your eldest son / my father

I cannot weep grandmother
cannot weep

Dreaming the Deathdream of the Mother

We walk with her between us on the street,
pausing to enter a house only when her legs
sag and her armpits by which we hold her
crack in the hot, dry night.
The airport is far away.

This is our family: the farewells have been said,
and we wept as our mother reminded us of changes
to come—"The Dutch airlines," for example, "are far
ahead of the others."

In the house a fragrance hangs in the air.
My brother sniffs softly. Marijuana, he says,
and I shake my mother awake into the street.
Mother, I whisper fiercely in her ear, What
shall I tell my lost wife?

Let me die, she answers, at home.
We look at each other and nod.
It is true, she will die soon.
The airport is far away.

A Jog for Jerry

Not that you talked that much
when we jogged that long summer
slowly   round the Abbey.

The neck is thinner, the larynx gone
the eye is darker with a dying song.

Nor did I know (did you?)
of the dark and secret lover.
Your mutant cells desired her.

The breath is useless, the larynx gone
the tongue is coated with a dying song.

You were mute, you were mated
as Papa said to that Old Bitch
Death, she took your love.

Spittle, spittle, larynx gone
rattle, rattle, dying song.

The monks are singing in the chapel.
No sound comes from their throats.
They are praying spittle rattle.

Spit a little before you're gone, Jerry—
rattle the Bitch with your dying song.

Strange Loops

(for E.M.)

There you stood in moose jaw that worried look or loop on
your face and we sat stunned in front of you would you choke
to death in the anguish that looped itself about you here on the
prairie your home where you had always been strange?

But you managed a deep gasp a breath of air filled your lungs
and your voice was suddenly stronger not less worried just
louder your brow was still worried but we too took deep
breaths he's going to make it we said to each other softly.

No one understood what you were trying to say the pain was
too much we couldn't hear anything except this hurts this
thought and the snake's tail in its mouth seemed to us an
excruciating circle but years later some would feel what you
meant.

But then your voice sank and the look on your face got strange
again and our brows too creased and something looped itself
around your brain and all our breaths were suddenly short
again all our brains were tightly squeezed as by a snake and
you smiled.

The applause rounded on you as you sat down still smiling
looking pained and some stranger rose to thank you and
your smile disappeared you looked down at the coiling floor
between your feet what was there that made you look suddenly
up and smile again?

For G.H.

Just lay your lyrics down, Poet,
Lay your lyrics down.
And sing your fearful song, Poet,
Sing your fearful song.

Your lyrics will live on, Poet,
Your lyrics will live on:
We'll sing your fearful song, Poet,
We'll sing your fearful song.

Diogenes at Agora

Diogenes at Agora

ok so you live in a glass jar beside a pine tree & wear nothing
but the holy string that you stole from that visiting brahmin
now sleeping curled up beside you the night after he said to
ask him anything & he would grant it & you said please sir
stand aside from the sun so i can continue reading & he drew
himself up as only a sadhu can naked as a jay bird but for that
sacred string his hindu logic split your head like the betel wad
he split with his teeth his lips red as blood & him covered with
chalky dust the brahmin slipped that string from his shoulders
& threw it eyes rolling in a frenzy on the tiles in front of you
& you staggered back as though his spittle had struck you &
fell to your knees bowing your head & kissing the string lying
on the agora & the holy man spoke again in a kind of singing
voice you had never heard a song so powerful it was that string
you now wanted so you offered the holy man a place to stay in
your jar & he scuttled up one side like a spider & slid down the
other in a stoned stupor had the song tired him after that it was
easy a piece of cake to pick up that string left lying on the agora
& now you can hardly wait … that power … that song … never
mind the glass jar …

Acknowledgements & Notes on the Poems

I want to thank Dennis Cooley for his sensitive, generous, and, above all, intelligent editing of these poems.

The following have appeared elsewhere in earlier versions: "Writing the Cutthroat" in *Grain* magazine; several "Cutthroats" and "Redbird & Cup" in *Rhubarb* magazine; "Mennomonk, The Poem" in *Grain* magazine; "Fuga per Canonem" in *The Rhetoric of Canadian Writing*, ed. Conny Steenman-Marcusse; "Lament" in *Number One Northern*, eds. Robert Currie and others; "Dreaming the Deathdream of the Mother" in *Poetry Canada Review*; "Diogenes" in *Transition* Newsletter #1.

"Cutthroat #8": "The embroidery of freudery" is the usual translation of Jacques Lacan's comment, *fofreudisme*, on psychoanalysis as practised in North America. See his *Ecrits*, translated by Bruce Fink, p.438.

"Cutthroat #10": Comet Hale-Bopp was clearly visible in Canada in March 1997.

"Cutthroat #13": Lines 3-5 play on a phrase in William Gass's *On Being Blue*, pp.89-90.

"Moment of Perfection": A doula is a trained birth-assistant, male or female, but not necessarily a midwife. The last two lines of this poem are an obvious parody of several well-known lines from Beckett's *Waiting for Godot.*

~